CHRISTMAS MUSIC IN THE BRITISH ISLES FOR CLASSIC GUITAR

PETER
WORLEY

WWW.MELBAY.COM

Preface

While compiling my first book for Mel Bay Publications, *Classical Guitar Tunes English Folk Songs* (30947M), I originally included "The Sussex Carol" as it was rooted in the English folk tradition. William Bay said that it might be better to include the carol in a separate book of British Christmas carols. Leaping at the opportunity to write a second book for Mel Bay, I ordered a copy of *The New Oxford Book of Carols* and began my research. My overall aim was to produce fresh arrangements of very well-known—dare I say, "tired"—melodies that I would want to play again and again, and also to present new holiday melodies to the player in a way that would make them shine.

The collection being British meant that I could draw upon the Welsh, Irish and Scottish traditions too. That said, I was struck by just how many well-known Christmas carols are found within the English tradition. England is the dominant player here, although it must also be remembered that many *English* carols were folk songs first, and only later were appropriated by England and Christianity. My instructions were to include only traditional carols, so no commercial or modern holiday songs were used. I did include one twentieth century composition by Gustav Holst that may not – strictly speaking – fit the bill, but the tune to "In the Bleak Midwinter" is so popular that it can just about pass for a traditional melody, so I hope you'll agree with my free treatment of the publisher's requirements in this case. It is also such a lovely tune that it's beauty alone surely qualifies it for inclusion.

I wanted to include many of the classic carols that everyone expects to hear around Christmas time, such as "Once in Royal David's City" and "The First 'Nowell!". I also wanted to present them in their familiar form so that they could be used in scenarios where the classic carols were called for. In a few cases, I transcribed some of the famous keyboard arrangements, retaining as much as I could of the classic voicings and harmonization that are often disappointingly absent in guitar reductions or simplifications.

To achieve this effect, I set the arrangement/transcription in an easy-to-play key such as G major but was left with the accompanying problem of it sounding too muddy and viscous. Rather than re-arranging the tune in a better-sounding key that would often be harder to play or would result in having to leave out certain notes that one would wish to retain—I opted to make use of the capo as I did in *English Folk Songs* (30947M). By placing the capo at the second or third fret I hope that you will find the arrangements of carols such as "O Come All Ye Faithful" and "Once in Royal David's City" satisfyingly complete and playable while avoiding harmonic viscosity. Where you place the capo—and whether you place it at all—I leave to the player's discretion.

In addition to providing the player with a standard treatment, I have often followed these with one that let my creativity off the leash. These treatments include some more jazzy harmonization (e.g., "Away in a Manger" and "Good King Wenceslas"), contemporary harmonization (e.g., "Sussex Carol" and "Ye Sons of Men") and some small sets of variations ("Tomorrow Shall Be My Dancing Day", "Thus Angels Sung" and "Remember, O Thou Man") and even a medley ("The Moon Shines Bright") made up of three different musical settings of the same carol discovered during my research; I found they ran into each other rather nicely.

In addition to familiar Christmas tunes, I also wanted to include a good number of lesser-known carols so I hope that you will also find a host of carols that you've never heard before but will want to play again and again. In seeking material for this book, I became acquainted with many beautiful tunes I'd never heard before—and found myself whistling them more often than the well-known ones; these include "Down in Yon Forest", "As I sat on a Sunny Bank", "In Those Twelve Days" and "Ye Sons of Men, With Me Rejoice", my personal favorite among my new discoveries.

I hope you enjoy playing my arrangements of well and lesser-known carols for family and friends for many Christmases to come.

Peter Worley
June 2021

Contents

Title **Page**

Alleluya: A Nywe Werk is Come on Honde

Capo on 2nd or 3rd fret

Fifteenth century, arr. Peter Worley

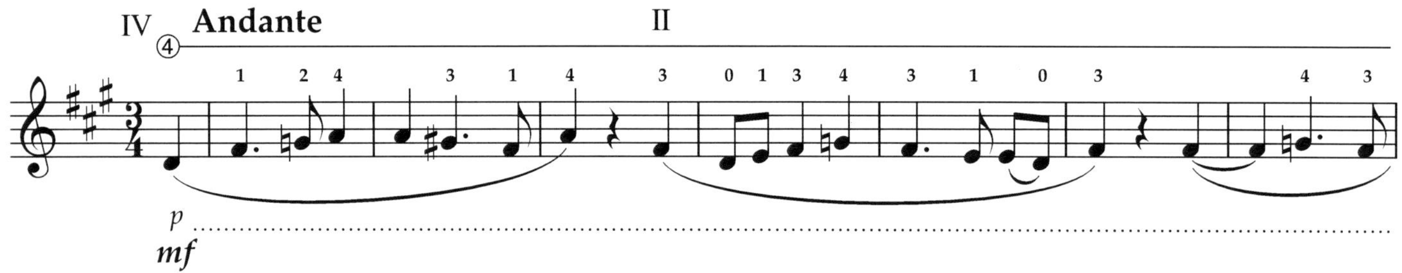

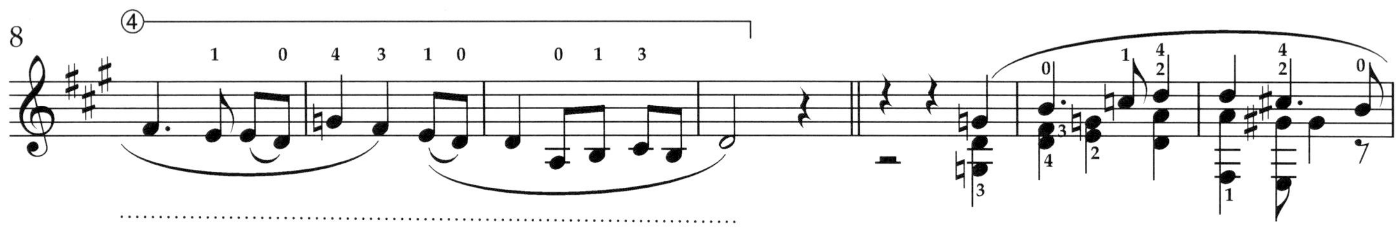

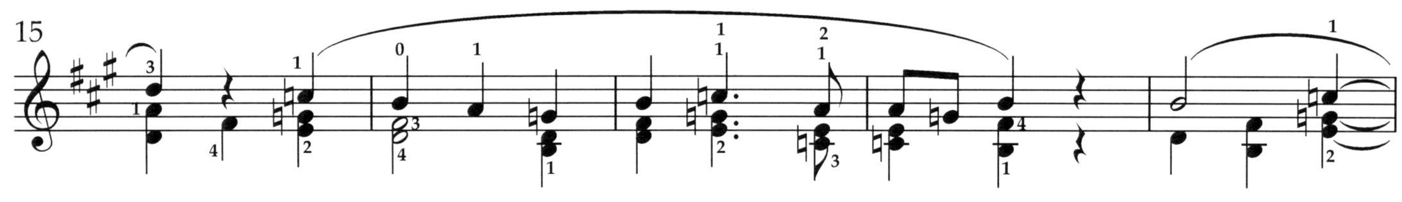

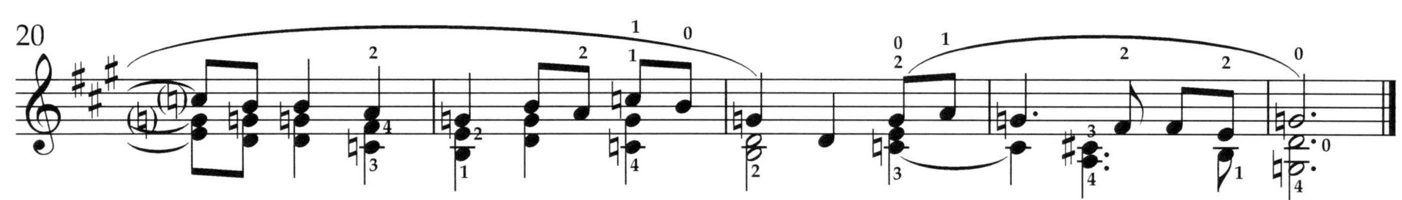

As I Sat on a Sunny Bank
(On Christmas Day in the Morning)

⑥ = D

Capo on 2nd fret

English trad. arr. Peter Worley

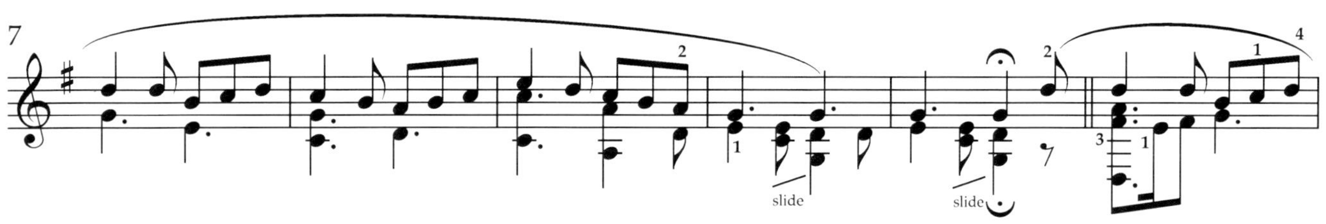

Angelus ad Virginem
(Gabriel, fram Heven-King)

⑥ = D

Thirteenth century, arr. Peter Worley

Adagio-andante

(stretch)

mf

II

II (stretch)

II

pont.

nat.

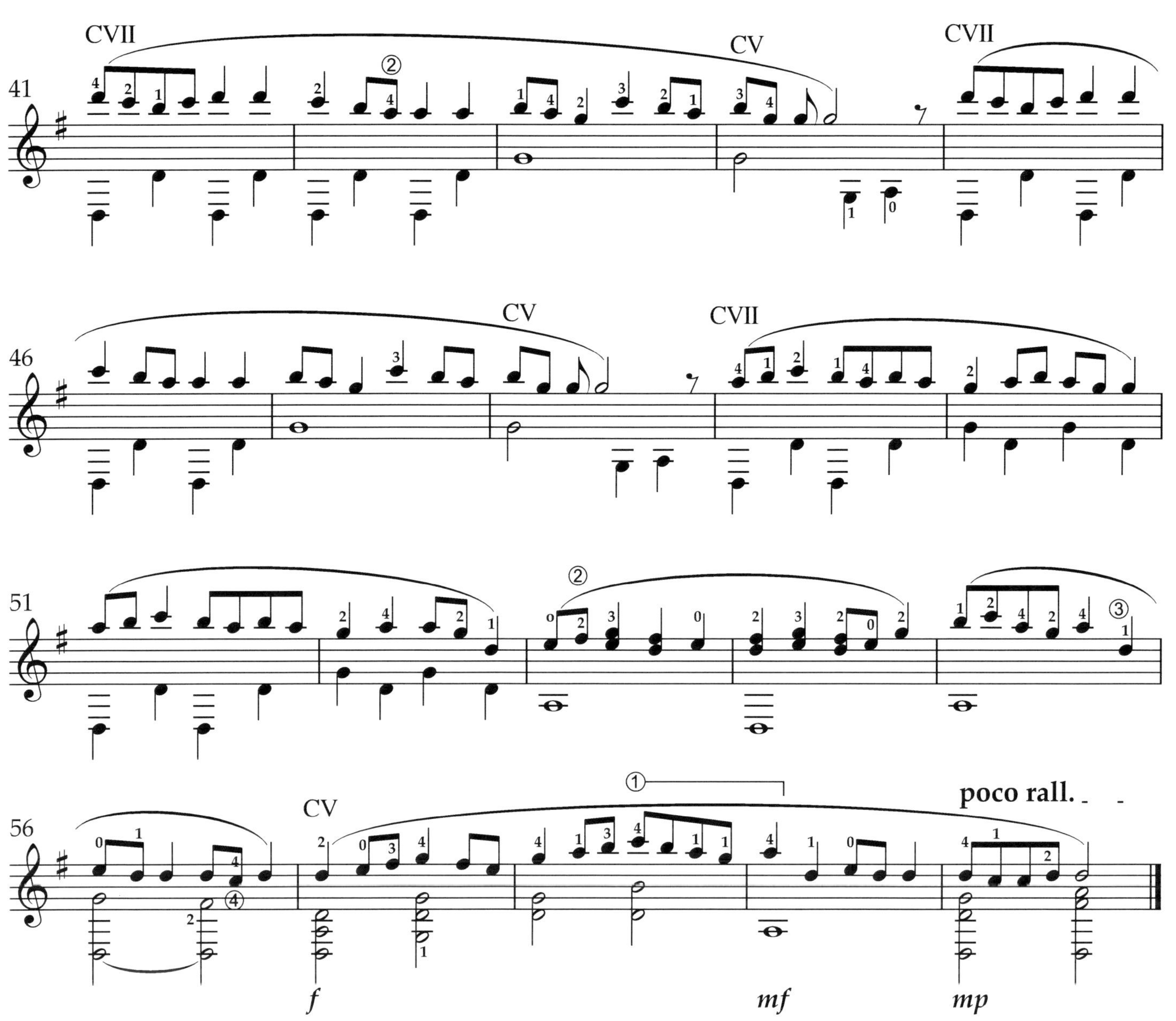
CVII
CV
CVII
CV
CVII
CV
poco rall.
f
mf
mp

Away in a Manger

William J. Kirkpatrick, arr. for guitar by Peter Worley

Baloo Lammy

⑥ = D

Scottish trad. arr. Peter Worley

Blessed Be That Maid Marie
(From William Ballet's Lute Book, 16th Century)

Capo on 2nd or 3rd fret

English trad. arr. Peter Worley

Andante-moderato-allegretto

Christèmas Hath Made an End (Well-a-Day!)

(The Gooding Carol)

⑥ = D
Capo at 2nd or 3rd fret

English trad. arr. Peter Worley

Ding! Dong! Merrily on High

English trad. arr. Peter Worley

Down in Yon Forest

(The Castleton Carol)

Capo at 2nd fret

English trad. arr. Peter Worley

God Rest You Merry, Gentlemen

English trad. arr. Peter Worley

Good King Wenceslas Looked Out

Fourteenth century, arr. Peter Worley (after Stainer)

Good People All, This Christmastime

(The Wexford Carol)

Capo on 2nd fret

Irish trad. arr. Peter Worley

I Saw Three Ships Come Sailing In

⑥=D

English trad. arr. Peter Worley

In the Bleak Midwinter

Gustav Holst, arr. Peter Worley

In Those Twelve Days

English trad. arr. Peter Worley

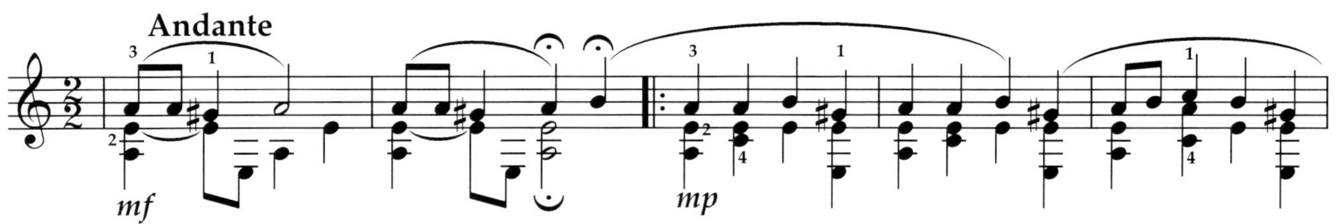

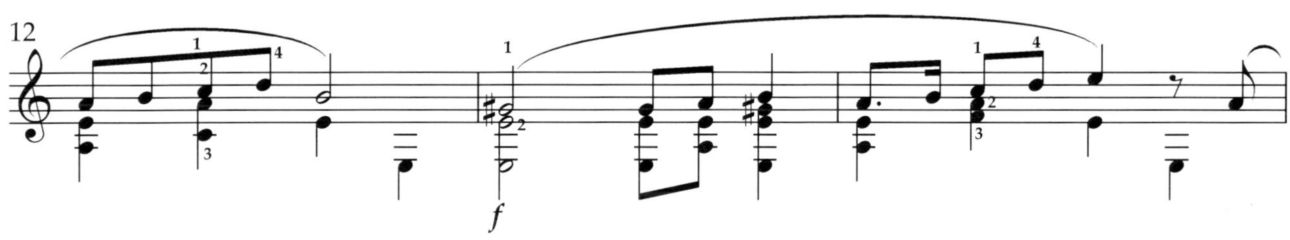

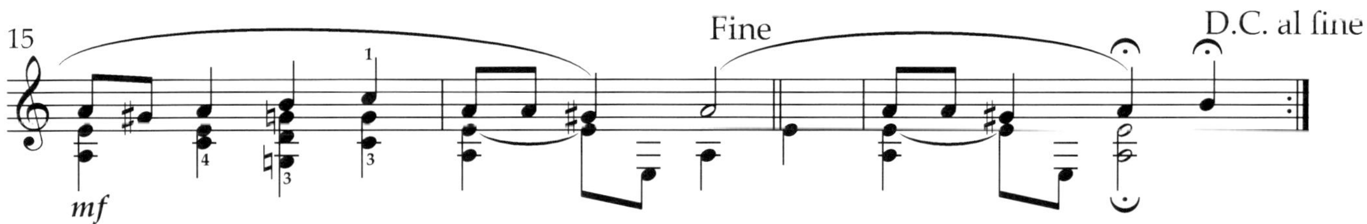

Joy to the World!

⑥ = D

William Holford, arr. for guitar by Peter Worley

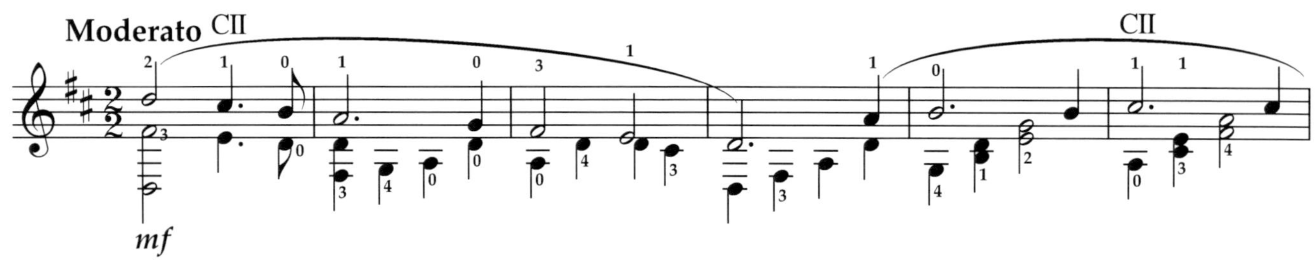

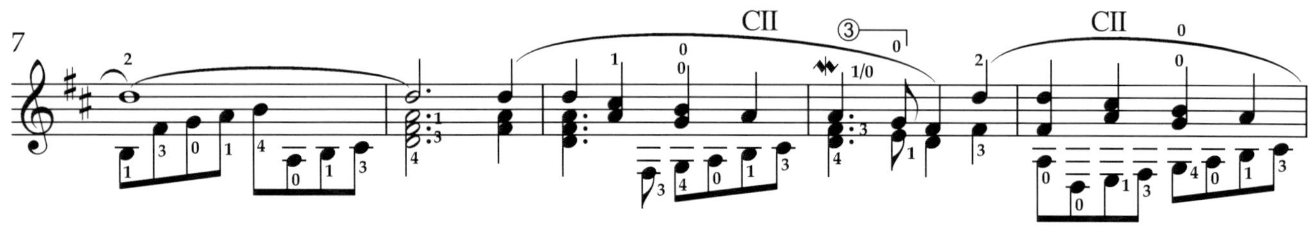

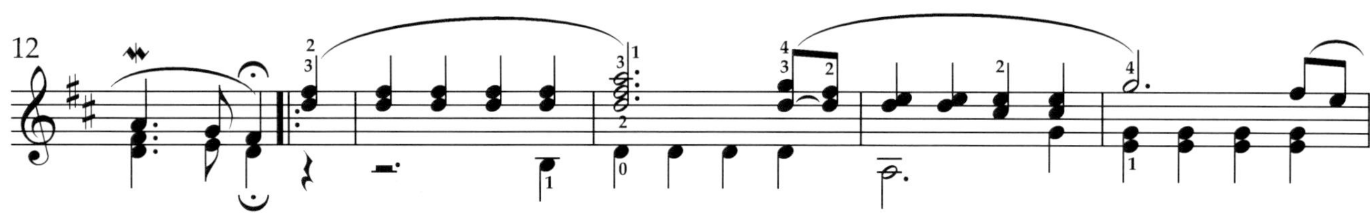

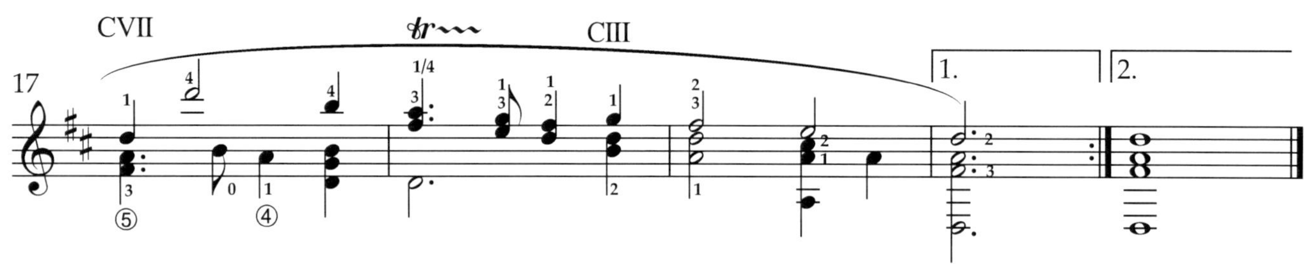

Lully, Lulla, Thow Littel Tyne Child
(The Coventry Carol)

Capo on 2nd or 3rd fret

English trad. arr. Peter Worley (after Sharp)

Andante-moderato

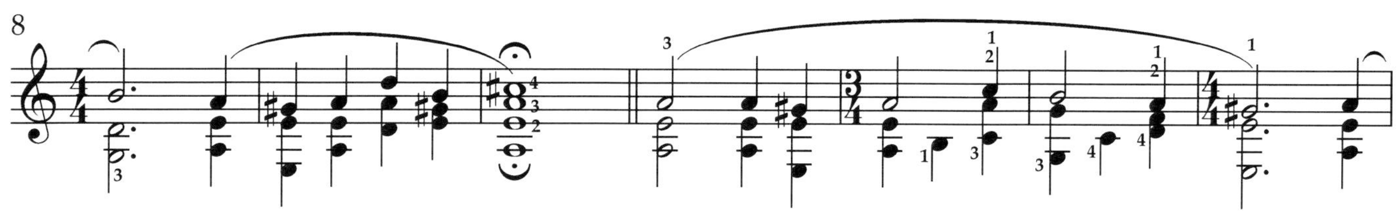

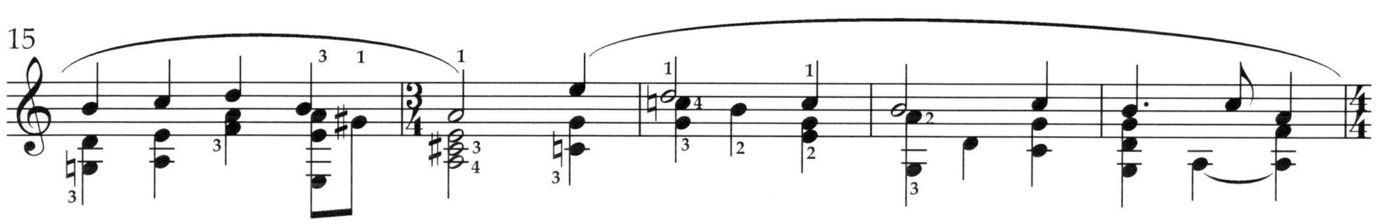

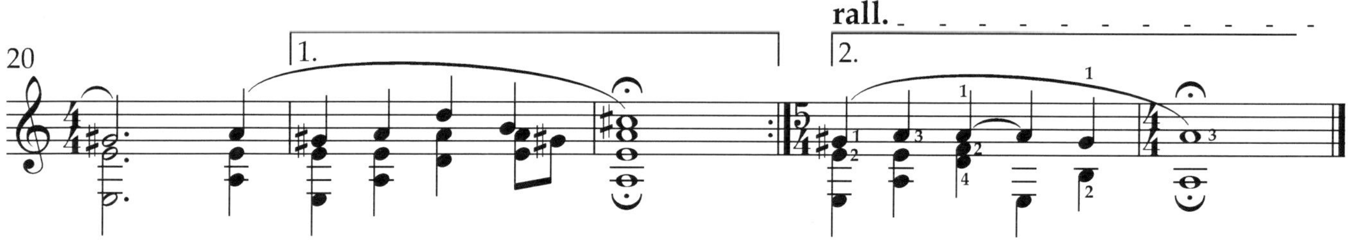

O Little Town of Bethlehem

English trad. arr. Peter Worley

O, Come, All Ye Faithful

Capo at 2nd or 3rd fret

Anon. arr. by Peter Worley after Thomas Greatorex

Lento-adagio

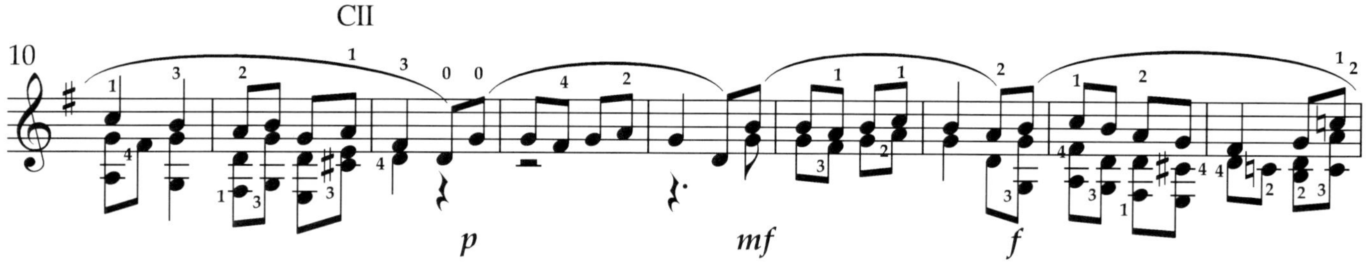

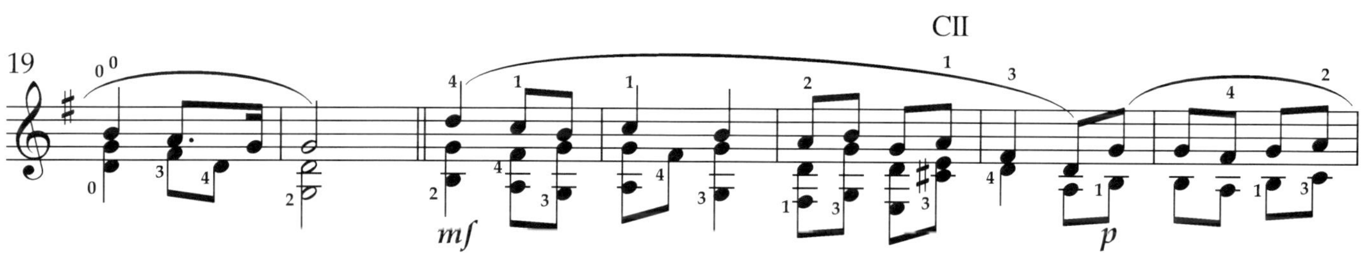

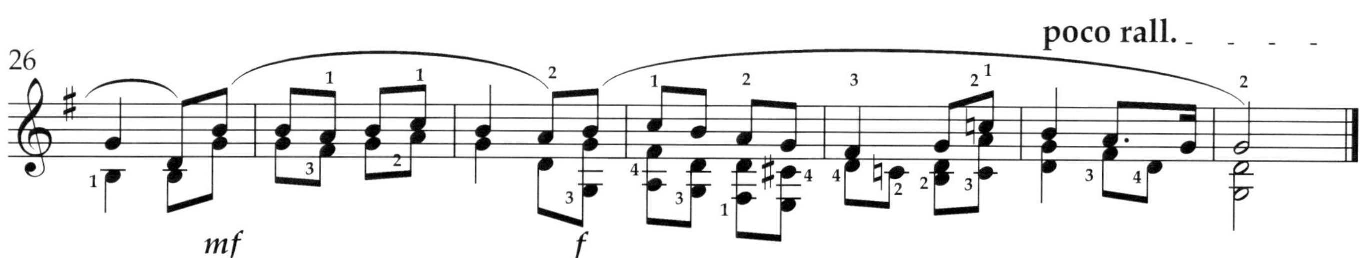

Oer Yw'r Gŵr Sy'n Methu Caru
('Deck the Halls')

Welsh trad. arr. Peter Worley

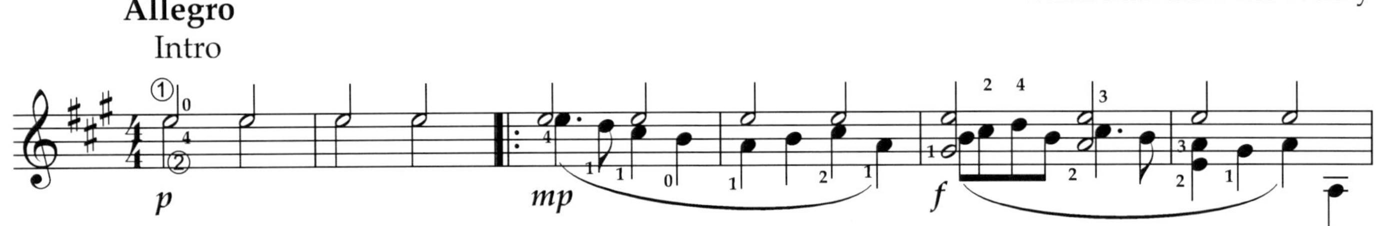

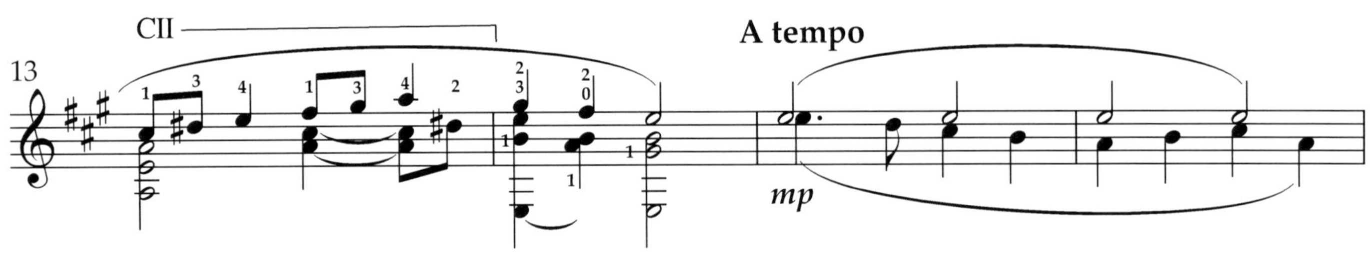

Once, in Royal David's City

Henry John Gauntlett, arr. for guitar by Peter Worley

Capo at 2nd or 3rd fret

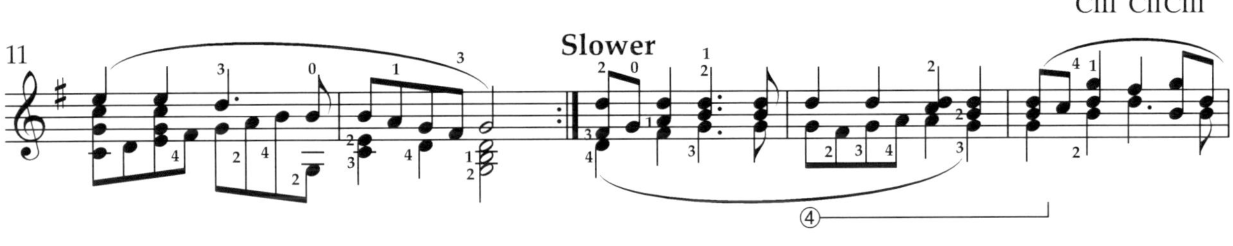

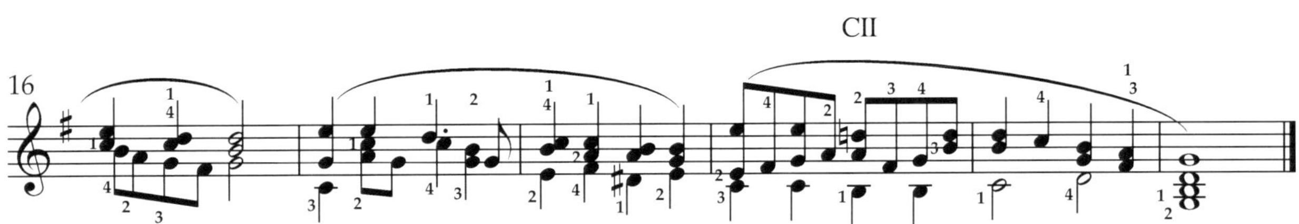

Rejoice and Be Merry

Capo at 2nd or 3rd fret

English trad. arr. Peter Worley

Allegretto-vivace-presto

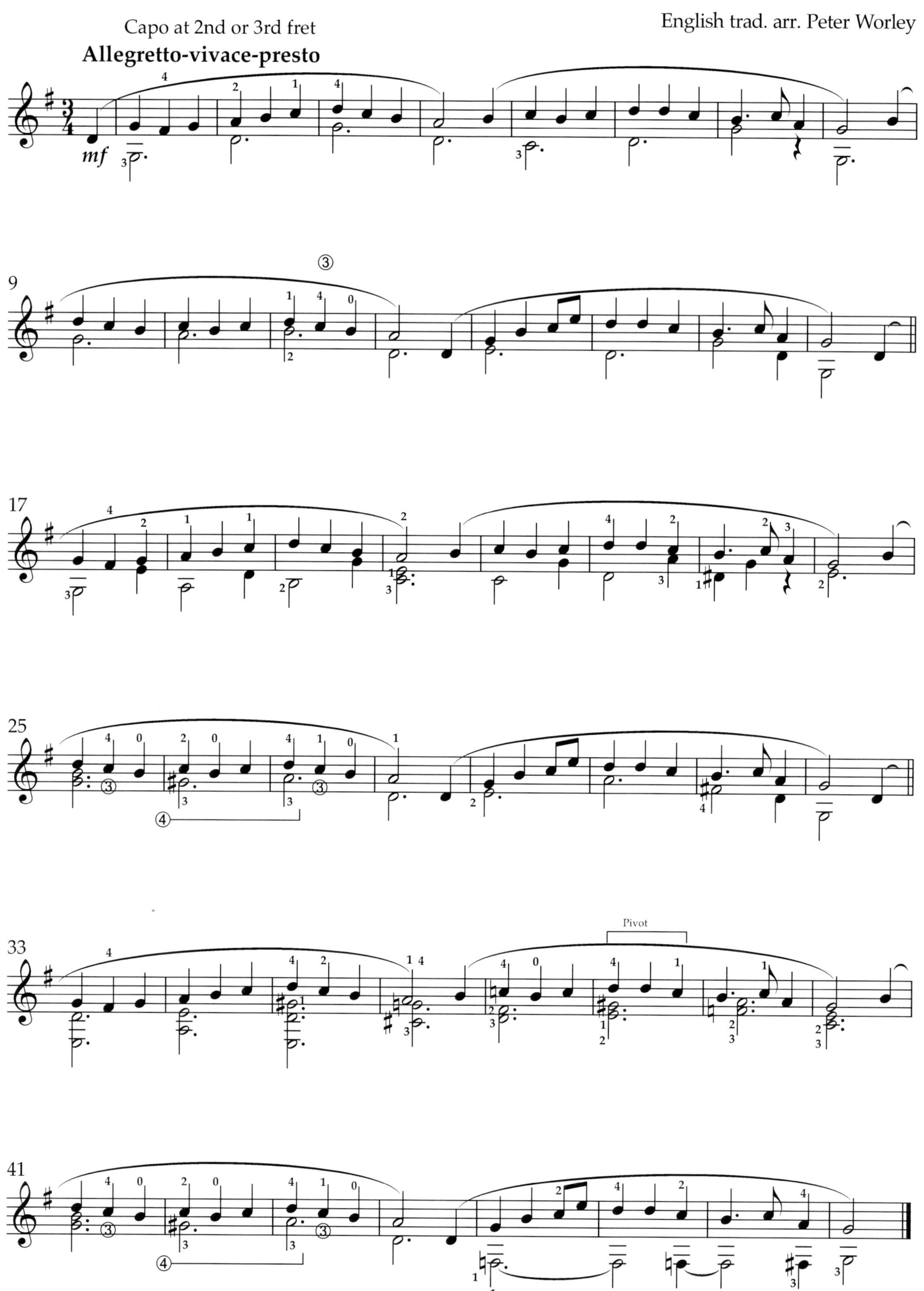

Remember, O Thou Man

⑥ = D

Capo at 2nd fret

Attributed to Thomas Ravenscroft, arr. Peter Worley

Andante

mf

Legato

mp

f

mp

poco rit.

A tempo

poco rit.

A tempo

rall.

mf

Rorate
(The Nativity)

Scottish trad. arr. Peter Worley

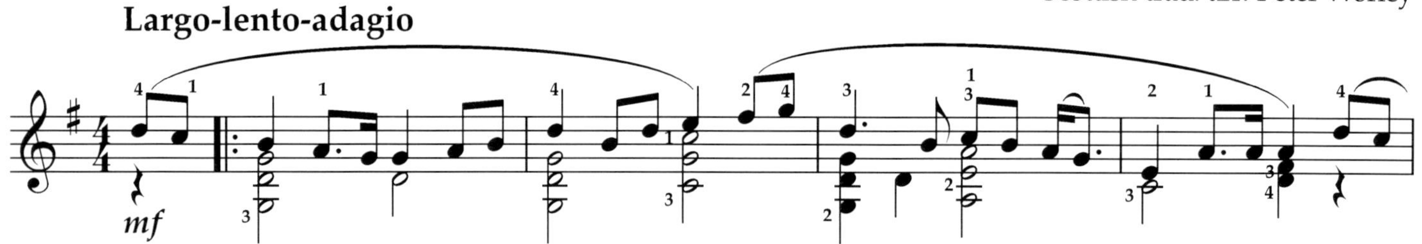

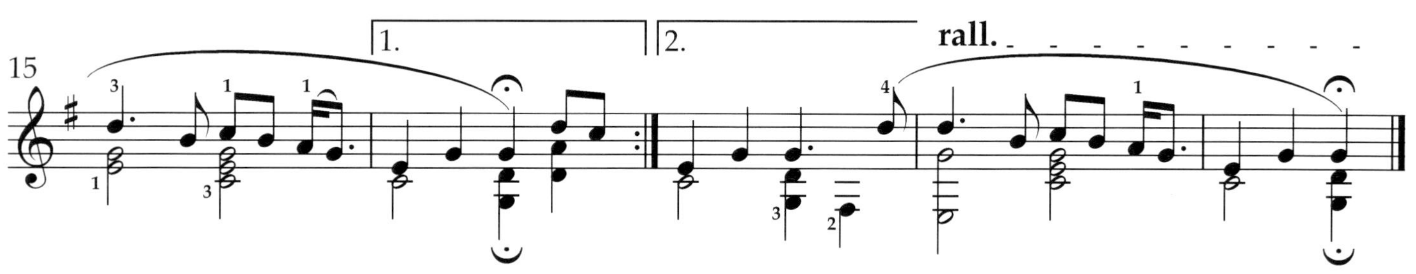

Sussex Carol

The Seven Rejoices of Mary

Capo on 2nd or 3rd fret

Irish trad. arr. by Peter Worley

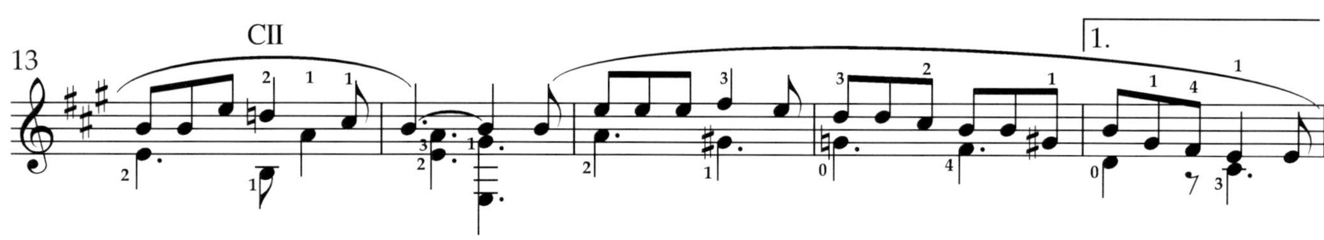

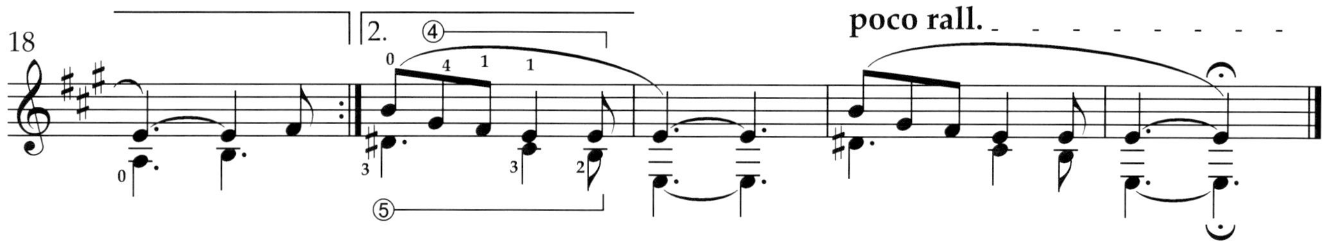

The Cherry Tree Carol

Capo on 2nd or 3rd fret

English trad. arr. Peter Worley

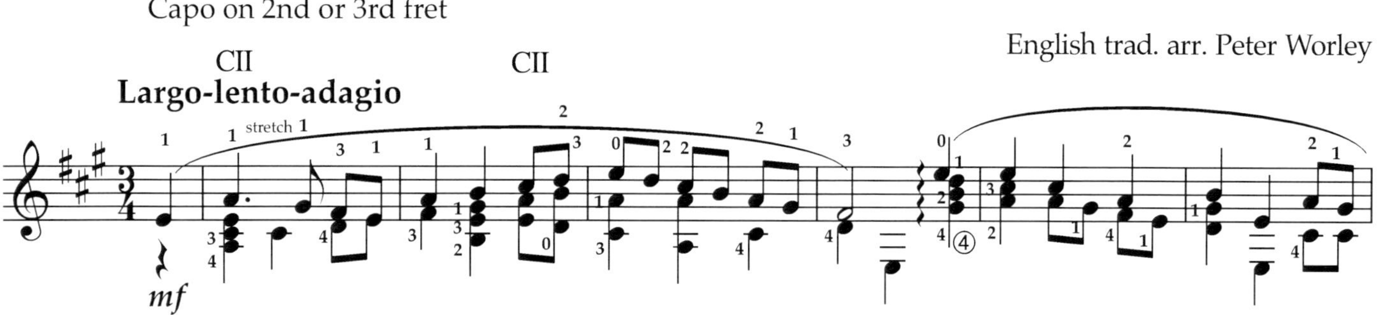

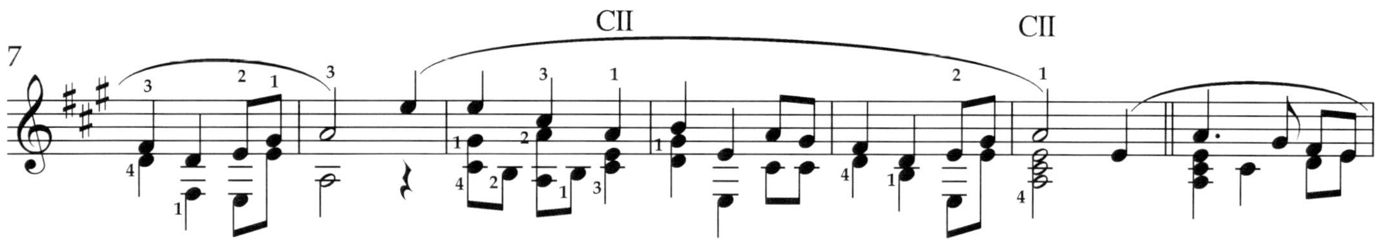

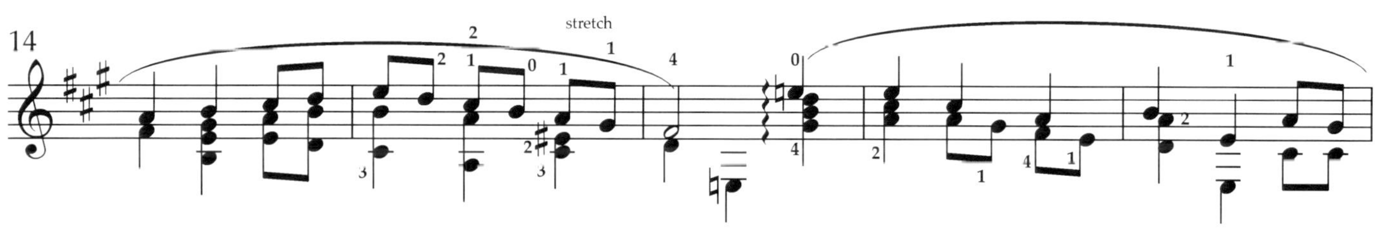

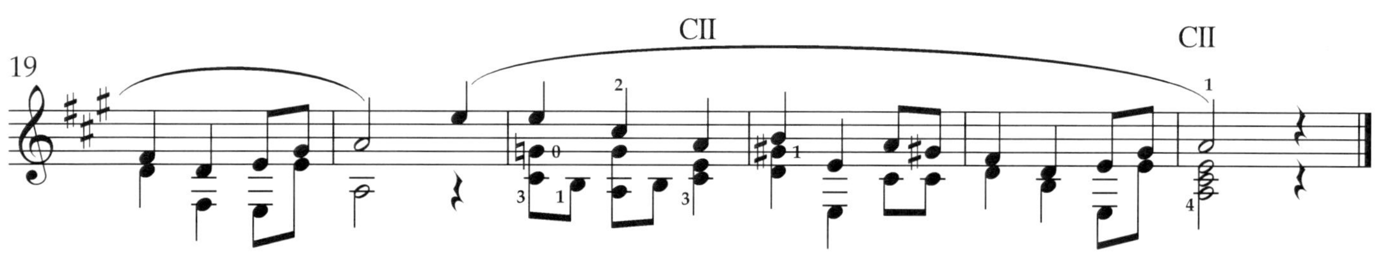

The Darkest Midnight in December

Irish trad. arr. Peter Worley

The Angel Gabriel from God Was Sent
(The Devonshire Carol)

English trad. arr. Peter Worley

The First 'Nowell!

English trad. arr. Peter Worley

The Holly and the Ivy

Capo at 2nd or 3rd fret

English trad. arr. Peter Worley

Intro

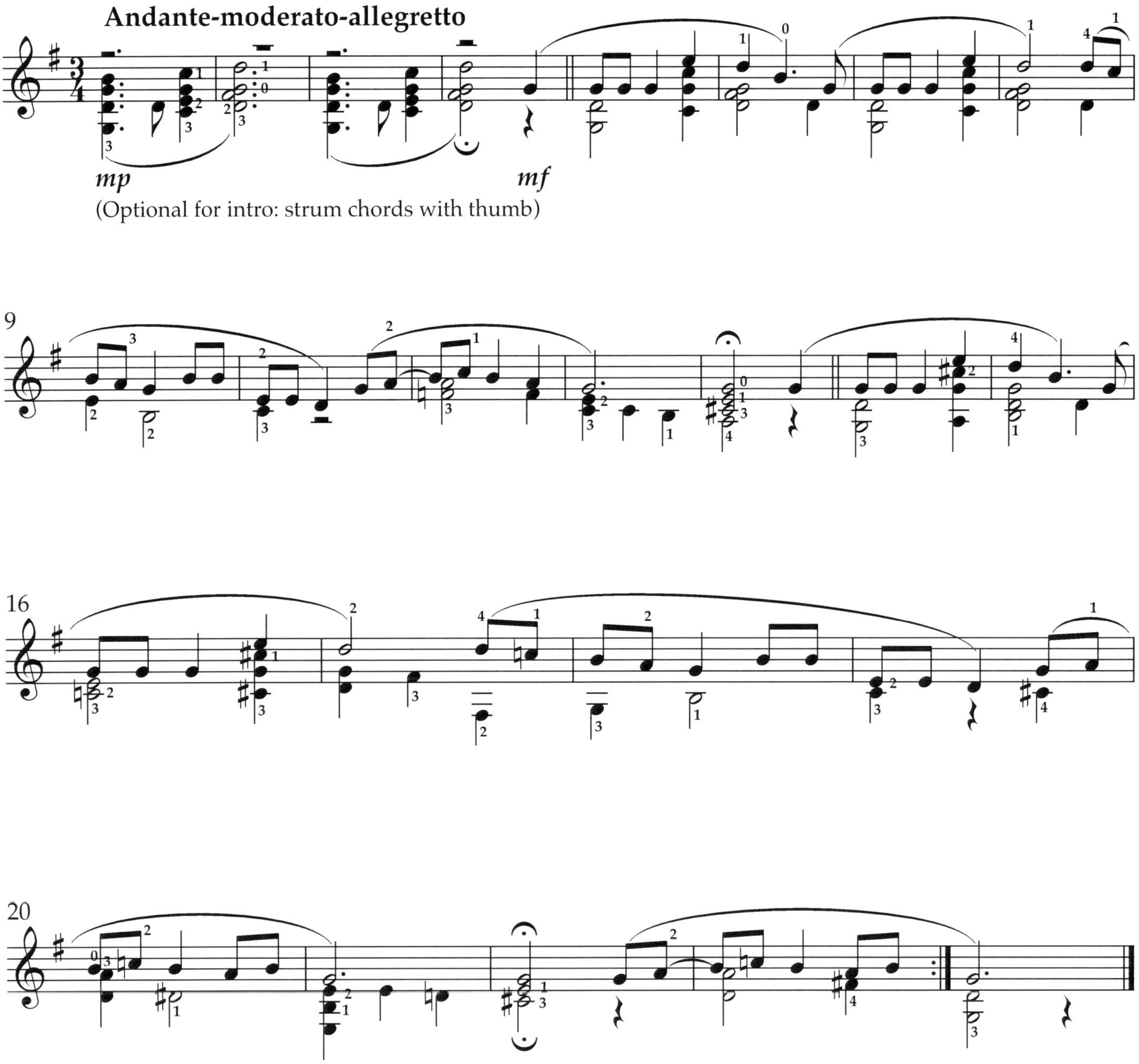
Andante-moderato-allegretto
mp
mf
(Optional for intro: strum chords with thumb)
9
16
20

The Moon Shines Bright
(A Medley of Musical Versions)

Capo on 2nd fret

English trad. arr. Peter Worley

Ther is No Rose of Swych Vertu

③ = F#
Capo on 3rd

Fifteenth century English, trans. Peter Worley

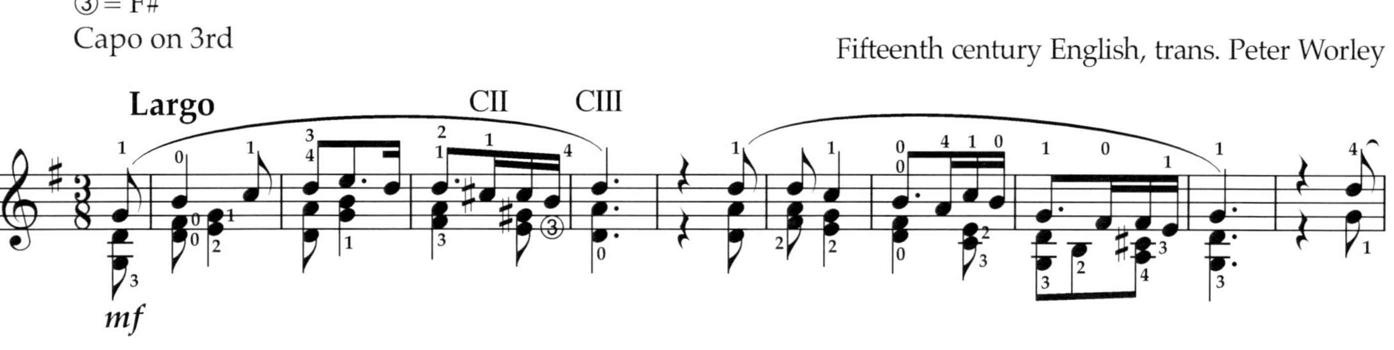

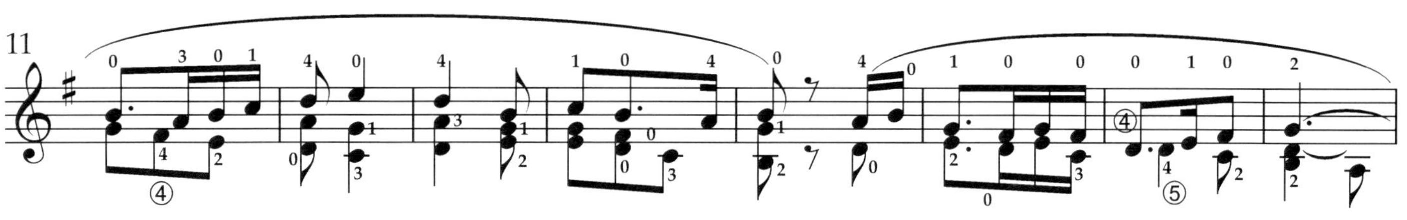

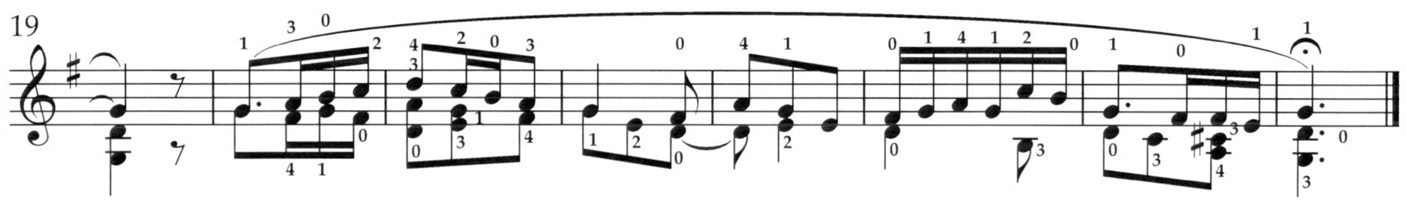

Thus Angels Sung

⑥ = D
[Optional: capo at 1]

Orlando Gibbons, arr. Peter Worley

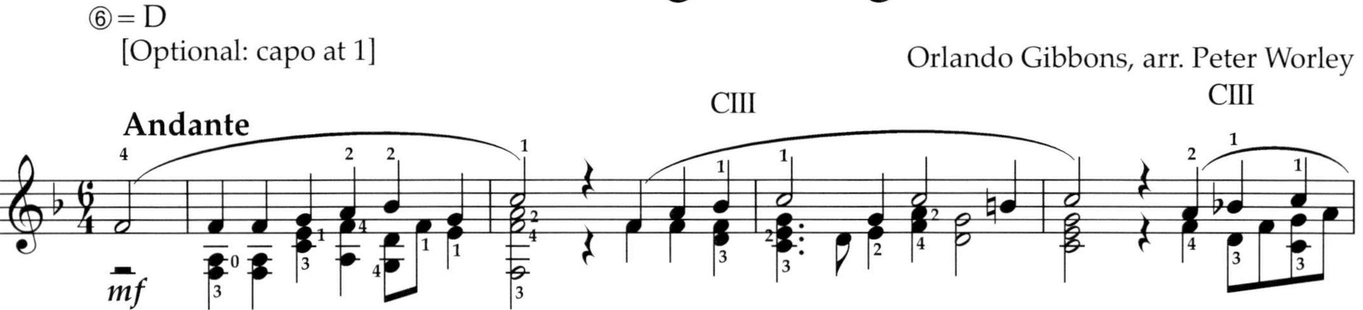

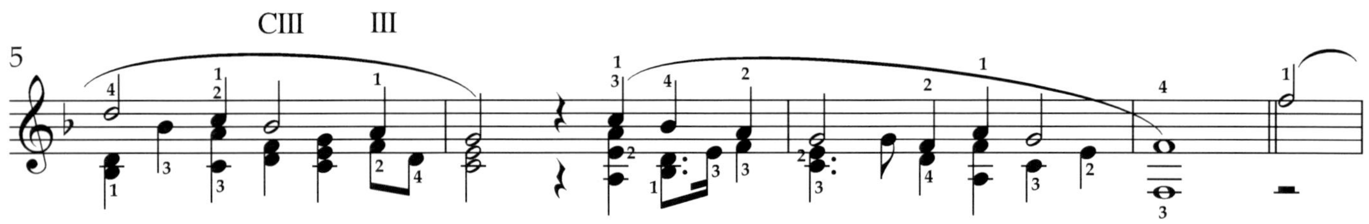

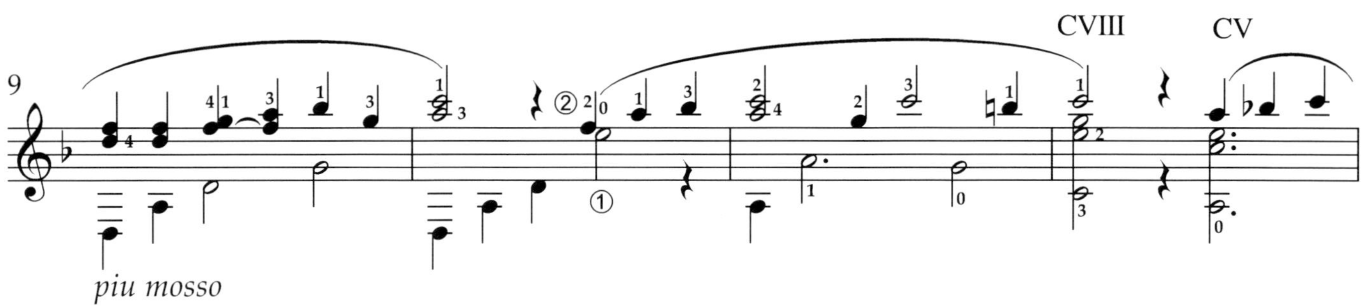

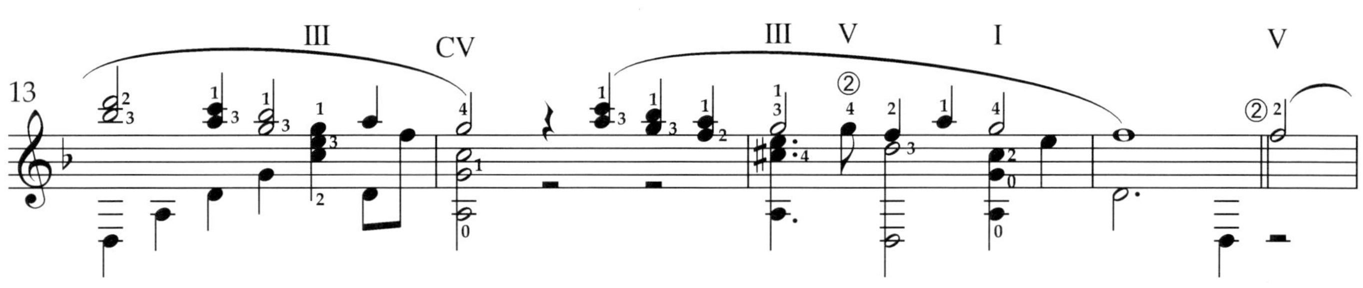

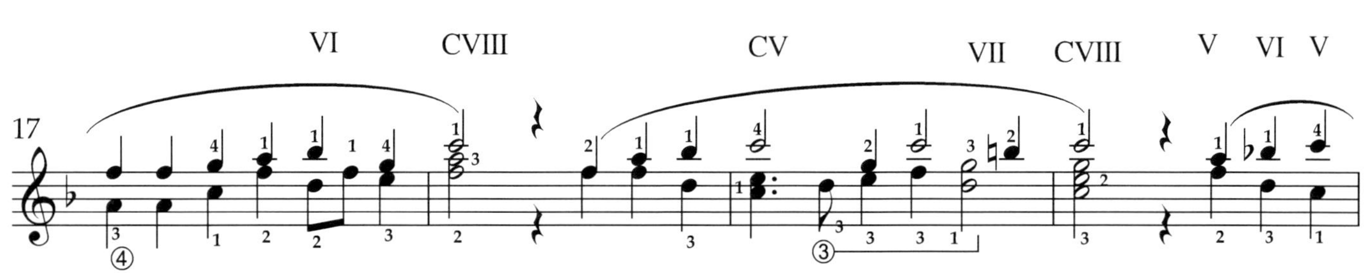

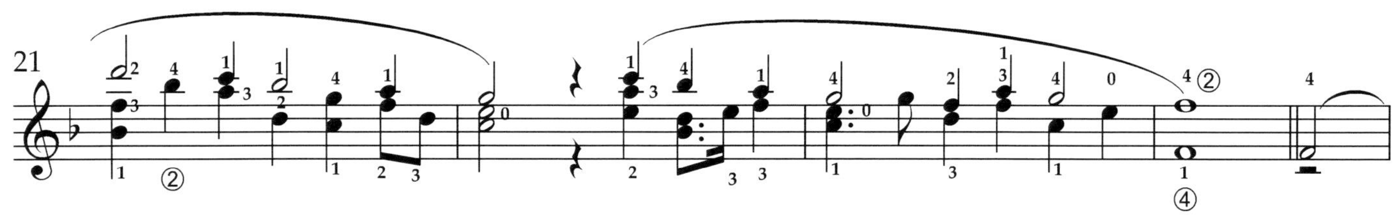
21

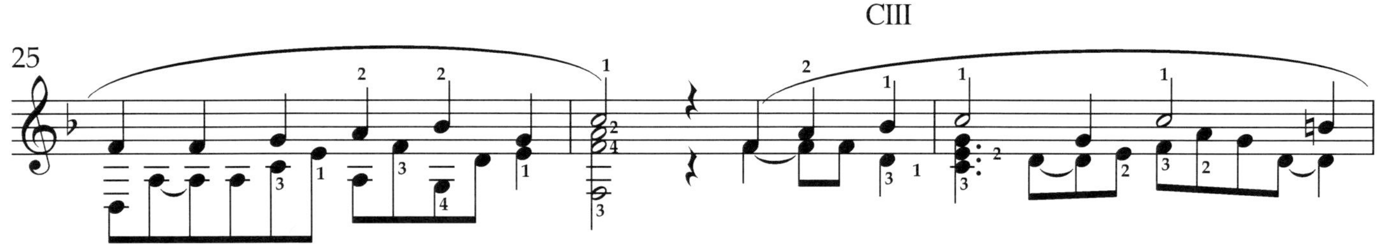
25
CIII

28

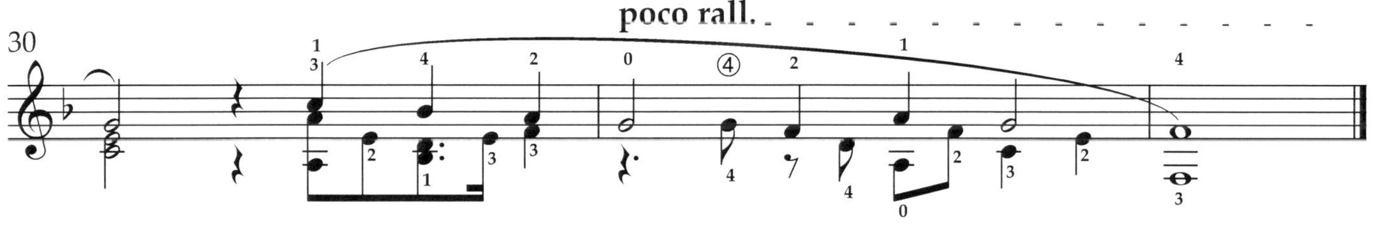
30
poco rall.

Tomorrow Shall Be My Dancing Day

⑥ = D
Capo on 2nd fret

English trad. arr. Peter Worley

Allegro (crotchet = 130 bpm)

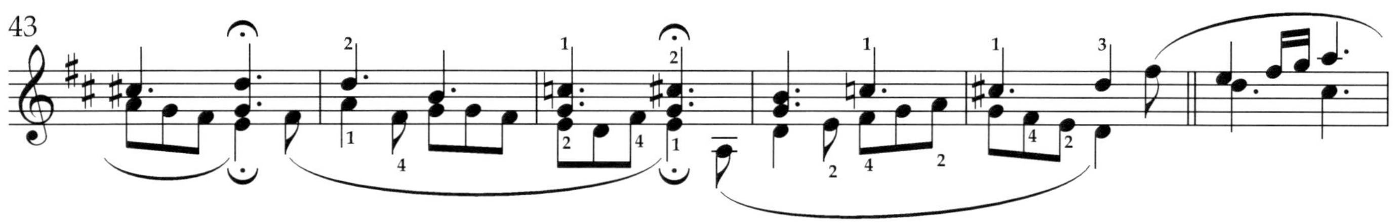
43

(Slower)
49

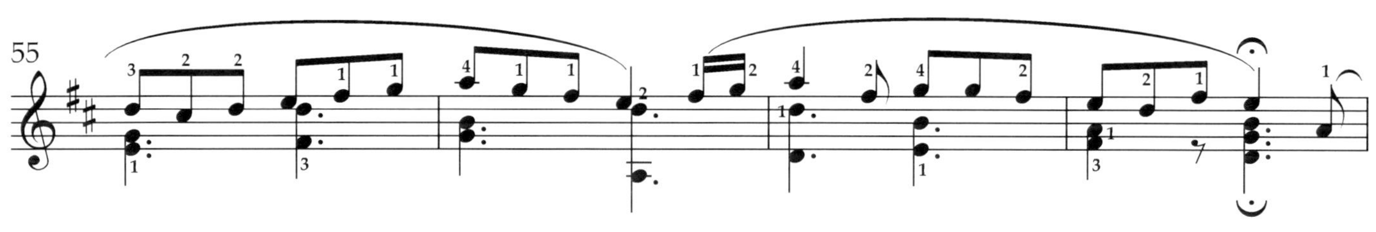
55

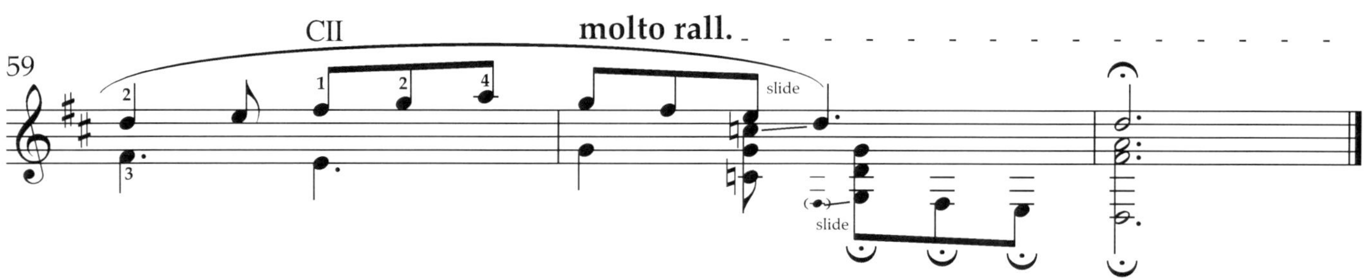
CII
molto rall.
59
slide
slide

Puer Nobis Nascitur

(Unto Us is Born a Son)

③ = F#
Capo on 2nd or 3rd fret

Trad. arr. Peter Worley

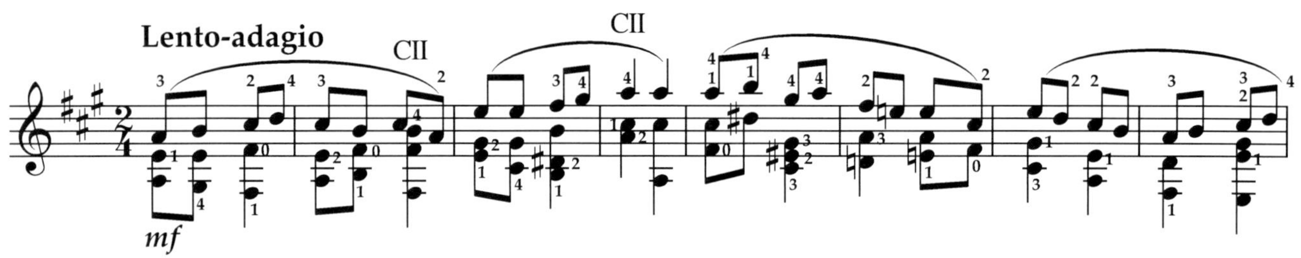

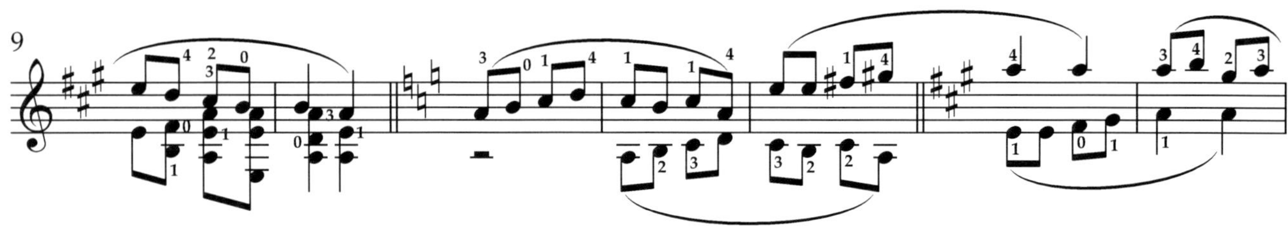

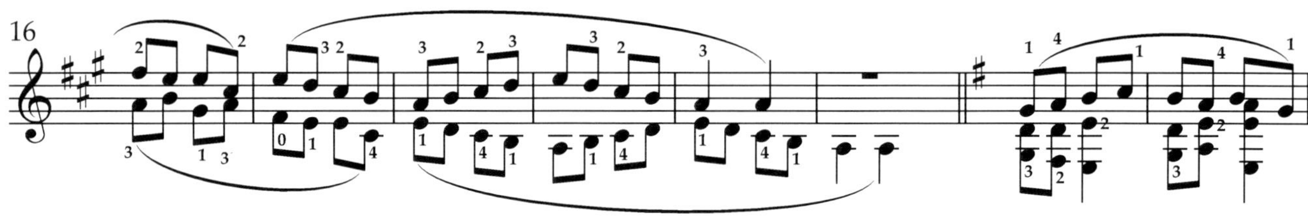

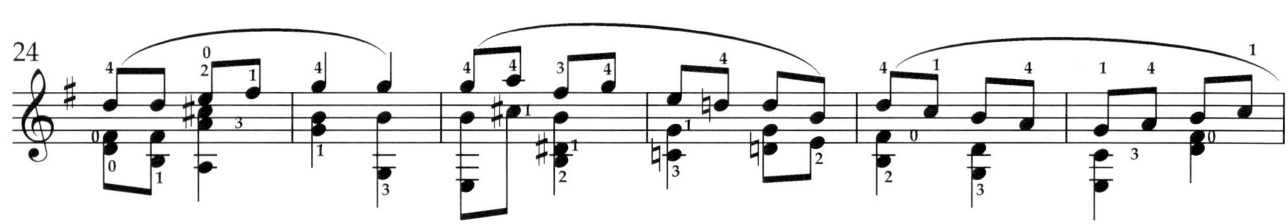

We Wish You a Merry Christmas

English trad. arr. Peter Worley

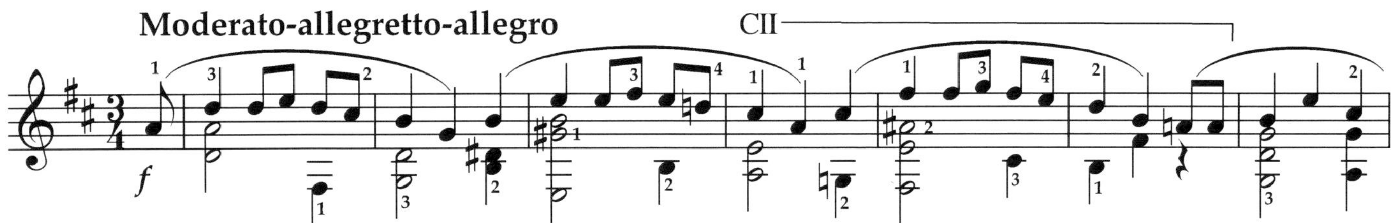

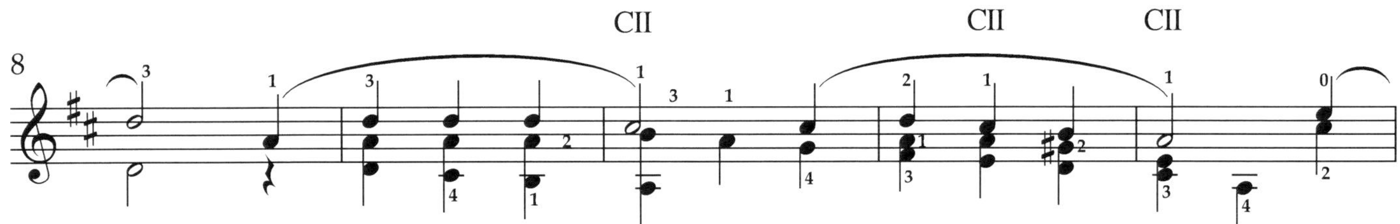

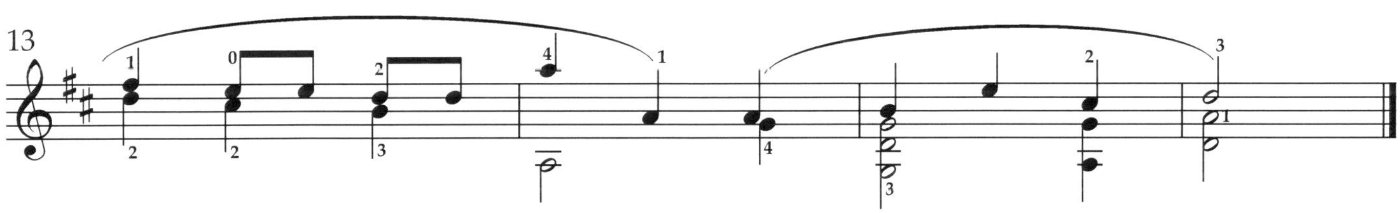

While Shepherds Watched Their Flocks by Night

Arr. Peter Worley (after Christopher Tye and Richard Allison)

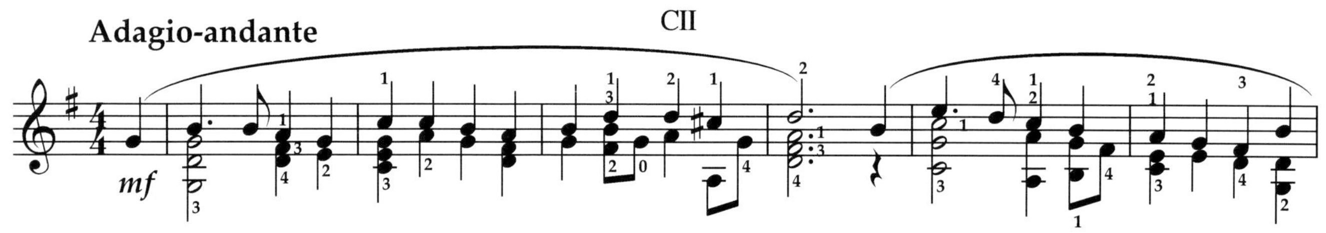

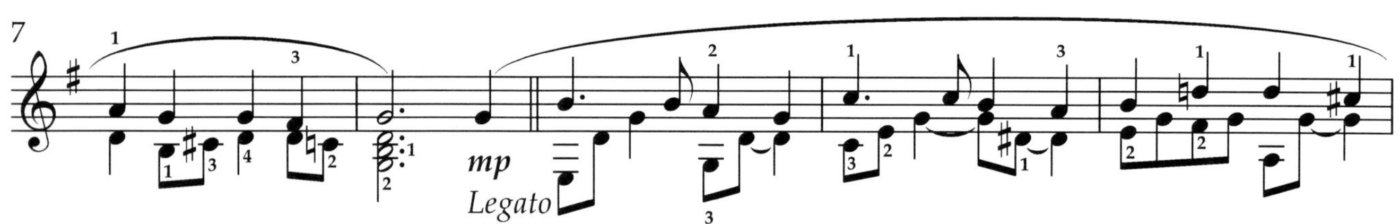

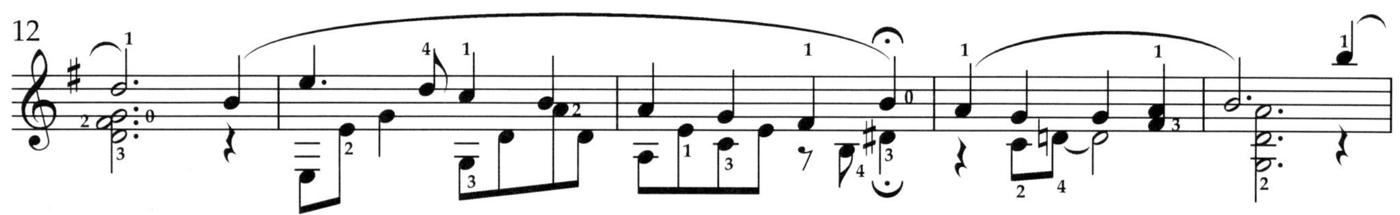

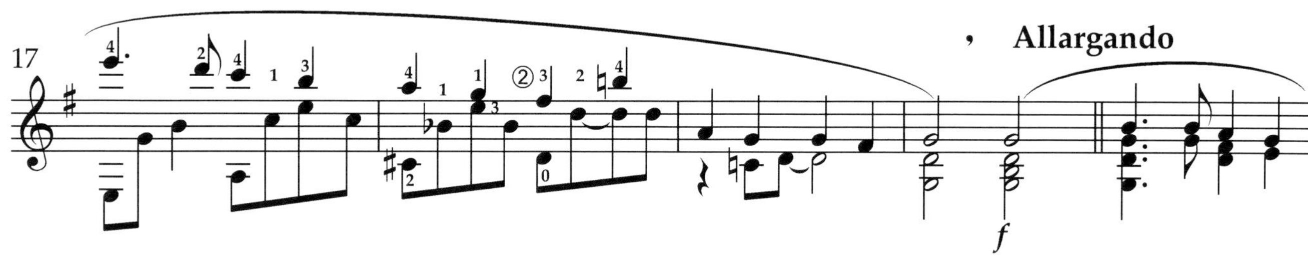

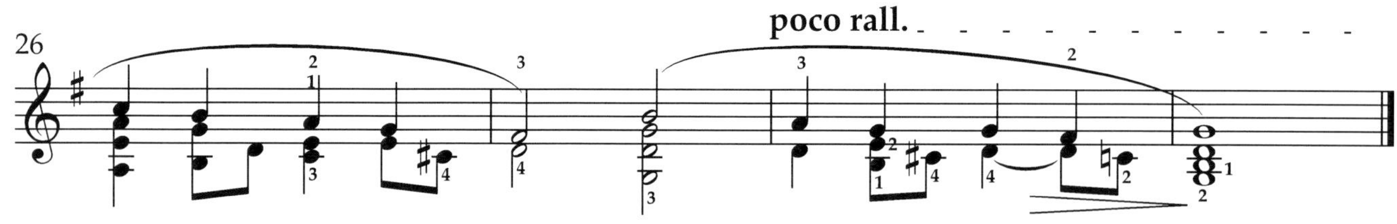

While Shepherds Watched Their Flocks by Night

⑥ = D

G. F. Handel, arr. Peter Worley

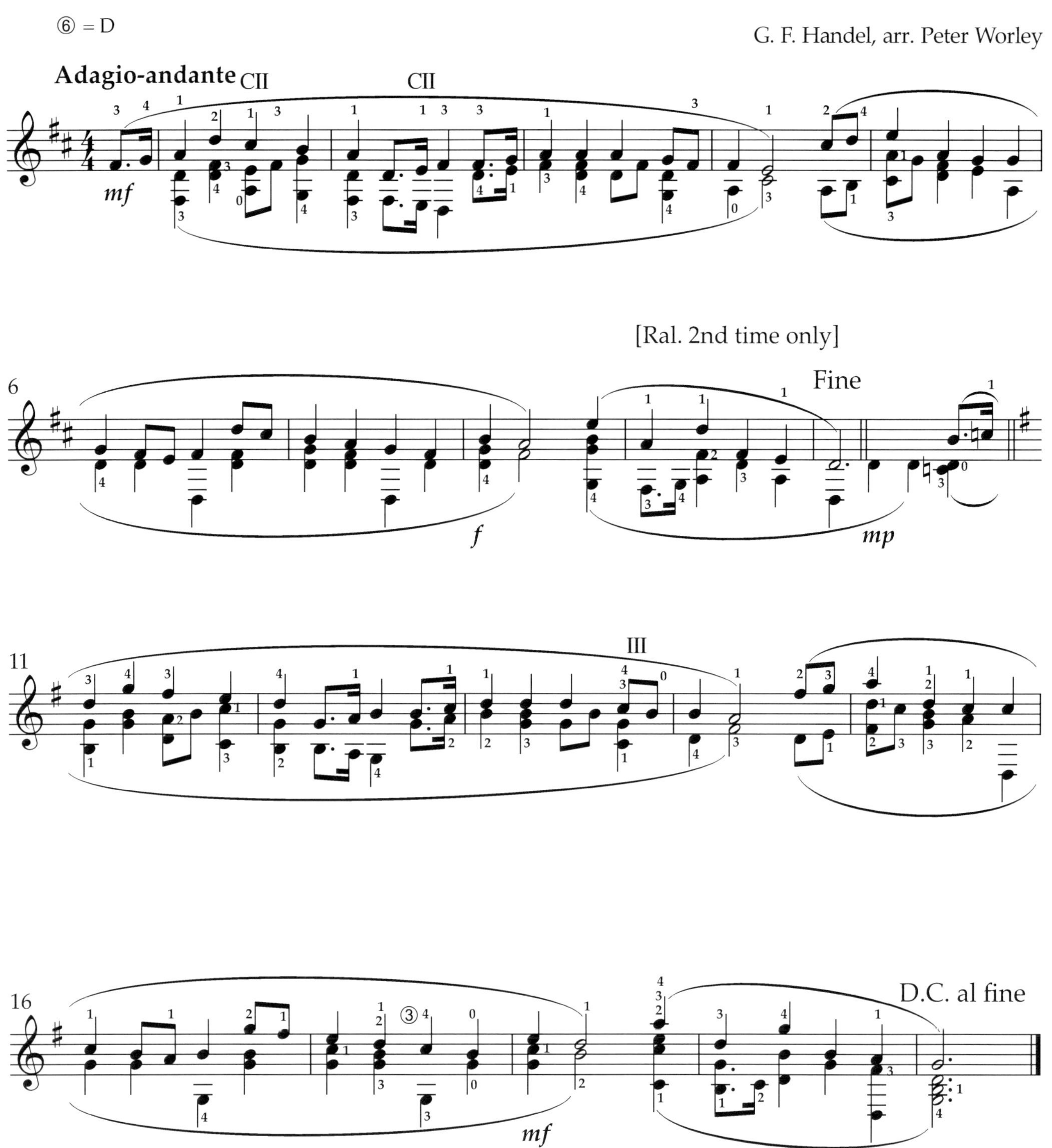

Ye Sons of Men, With Me Rejoice

Irish trad. arr. Peter Worley

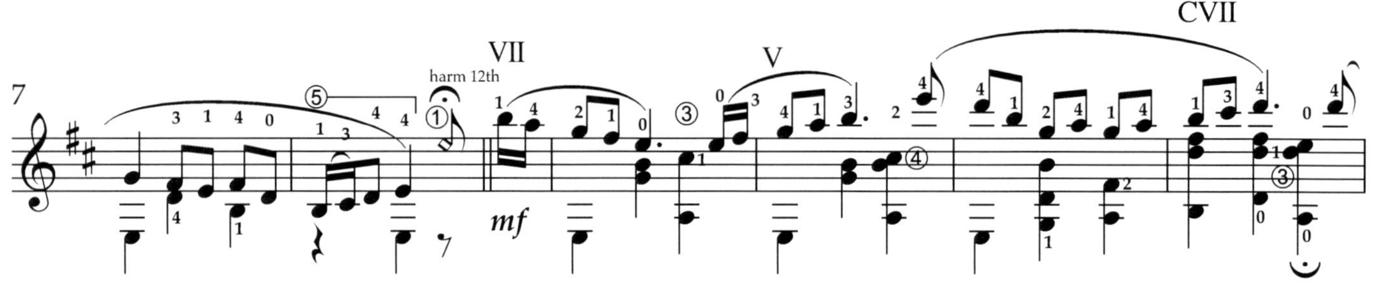

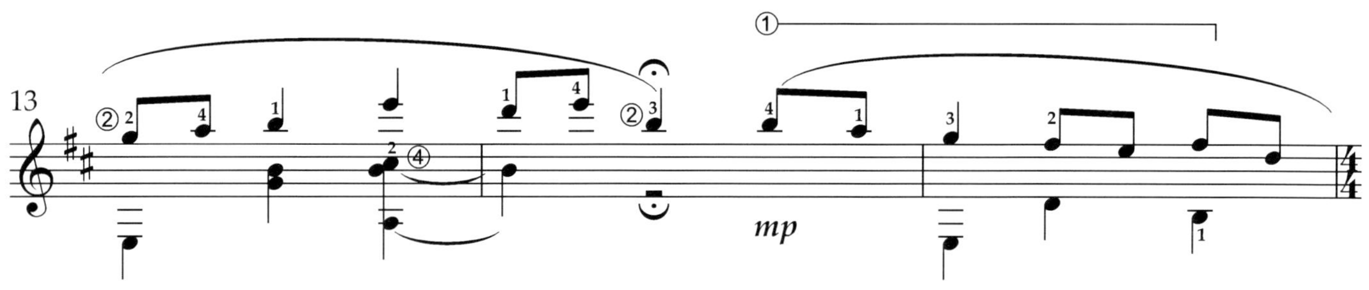

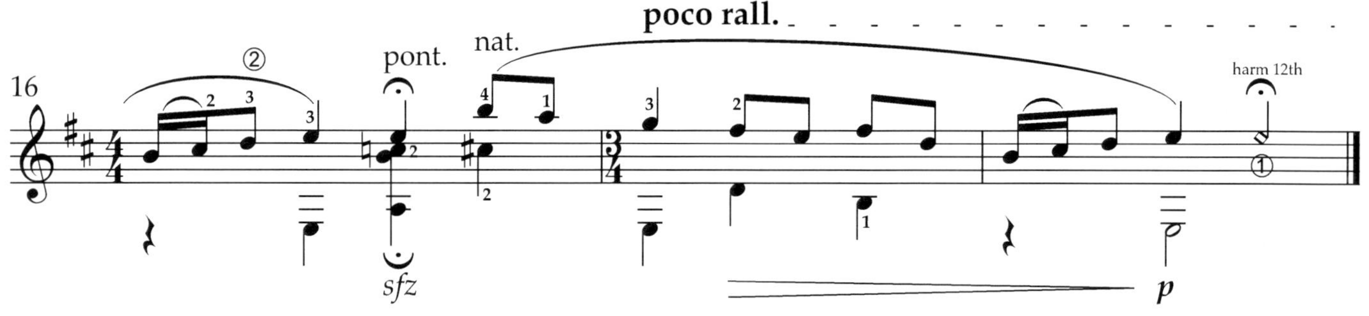

Joseph, Being an Aged Man Truly

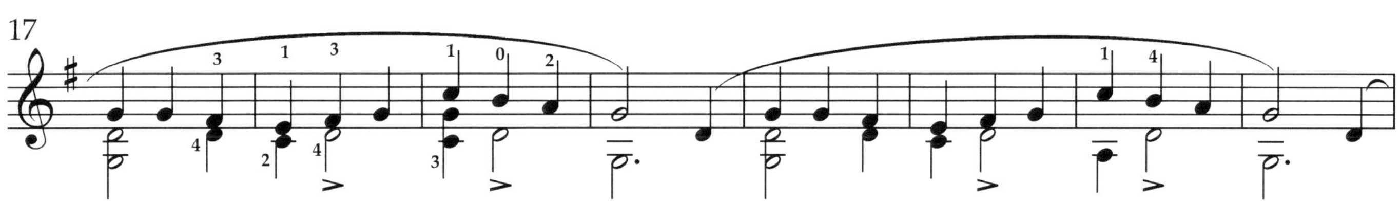

25

poco rall.

Let All That Are to Mirth Inclined

English trad. arr. by Peter Worley